Santa's

Christmas

Message

Written by

Alfred "Alfie" Weltmann

Images courtesy of cardcow.com

I dedicate this book to my son Alex, who reminds me every day, what is important and to Larisa, who has been my support through difficult times, and last but not least,
to His Honor, Judge P.J. Toal without whose encouragement, this story would never have been completed.

Hello everybody. I'm so glad you came.
I know who you are and you all know my name.
You're Peter, you're Betty, you're Sue and you're Paul.
I used to visit you when you were small.

Now I know that you'll remember me.
I used to put presents under your tree.
You used to ask for so many things.
Remember the presents I used to bring?

But now you're all older and it's that time again,
To go where I'm going and to be where I've been.
How do you do it the people all ask?
So many places to go, must be quite a task.

So listen my children and I'll tell you a tale,
Of a place way up north, from the pole,
where I hail.
A place that's so cold that we all stay inside,
Making the toys for our annual ride.

We work thru the day and all thru the night,
Preparing the toys for our Christmas flight.
The elves and I and all the reindeer,
Have all worked so hard for this day of the year.

I've read the reports from your moms and your dads.
I know who's been good and I know who's been bad.
Now this is the season overflowing with cheer.
We've waited and waited, now Christmas is here.

I've gotten the phone calls and letters you've sent,
I've gotten your messages, one hundred percent.
Your emails and texts, I've read every word,
You wouldn't believe all the things that I've heard.

Zach wants a baseball, Jake wants a bat,
Nicole wants a puppy, and Larisa a cat,
A video for Alex, a TV for Sam,
A ring for Julia, a new dress for Pam.

Now everything's wrapped and everything's packed.
Everything's straightened and everything's stacked.
I really must hurry I really must run.
It's time to get going, everything's done.

We load up the sled, to the brim full of toys,
In order to bring them to all girls and boys.
I hop in my sled and I'm off in a wink,
And I'm at your house before you can blink.

From rooftop to rooftop down chimneys galore,
I gather the presents round the tree on the floor.
Some warm milk and cookies, a snack here and there,
Makes the wind and the cold a bit easier to bear.

Then up thru the chimney and onto my sled,
I dust off the soot, fix my hat on my head.
I'm off once again to the house down the street,
Again down the chimney till my work is complete.

Now not every house has a chimney today.
No need to worry, I'll find a way.
The stairs or the window, the door if I must,
I won't miss your house, that you can trust.

From New York to Paris and from Paris to Rome.
I fly round the world till I come to your home.
To all of the homes, all the places I've seen,
All of the children from toddlers to teens,

They're all fast asleep keeping warm in their beds,
And dreams of Christmas filling their heads,
Of gifts that await and family they'll see,
As they'll all gather round their beautiful tree.

Stockings are hung everywhere that I go.
I still fill them with gifts like I did long ago,
With toys and with candy, perhaps a surprise,
I wish I could see the joy in their eyes.

And although I may do all I'm able to do,
I really don't mean to forget about you,
And though sometimes,
Someone, may slip through the cracks,
There's always next year, you know I'll be back.

Not much has changed in hundreds of years,
So many children on both hemispheres.
Some kids are happy there are some who are not,
I do the best that I can with whatever I've got.

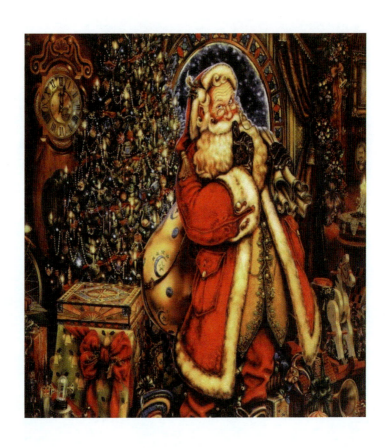

And because of the millions of kids that I see,
I hope you won't be angry with me,
If some of the things that you've asked me for,
I'm unable to bring, please don't be sore.

With all of the things that I need to do,
It's my turn to ask a little something of you.
If you were to help others, I know you'll agree,
Things would be made so much easier for me.

So remember my children the things we must do
Be good to each other and remember this too,
Though this is a special time of the year,
To think of our loved ones both far and near.

Kindness and love are where peace begins,
And when we're nice to each other everyone wins.
Do what you can to help those in need,
Whether it's kindness or clothing, or people to feed.

Be kind to your family, your neighbors and friends,
The joy that it brings, the pain that it mends.
And if everyone helped just 2 or 3,
Think what a wonderful world this would be.

This is what Christmas is truly about,
Doing for others, without question or doubt.
So help those around you, those less fortunate than us,
And when you're upset, don't make such a fuss,

And instead of being nice just one day a year,
Fill every day with laughter and cheer,
And when mom or dad ask you to clean up your rooms,
Pick up your toys for I'll be seeing you soon.

Santa
Wishes Everyone
A Very
Merry Christmas

Made in the USA
Charleston, SC
08 August 2014